IMAGES
of America

MONTCLAIR
A POSTCARD GUIDE TO ITS PAST

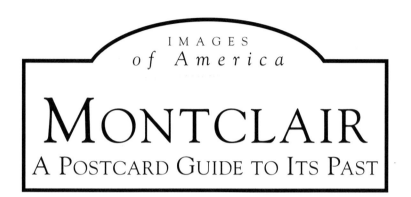

IMAGES
of America

MONTCLAIR
A POSTCARD GUIDE TO ITS PAST

Philip Edward Jaeger

ARCADIA

First published 1998
Copyright © Philip Edward Jaeger, 1998

ISBN 0-7524-1224-8

Published by Arcadia Publishing,
an imprint of Tempus Publishing, Inc.
2 Cumberland Street, Charleston SC 29401.
Printed in Great Britain

Library of Congress Cataloging-in-Publication Data applied for

To my aunt, Ruth Hopper,
who gave me a love of history at an early age,
and to my wife, Jean, who gave me the time to pursue it at a later one.

Contents

Acknowledgments   6

Introduction   7

1.   Background   9

2.   Transportation   11

3.   Business Districts   25

4.   Education   41

5.   Churches   59

6.   Lodging and Leisure   71

7.   Residences and Streets   85

8.   Scenes around Town   113

Select Bibliography   128

Acknowledgments

Appreciation is gratefully extended to Jack Chance and Roy Shepard, respectively Montclair's first and current township historians, for sharing their knowledge of the town's history with me and for making many insightful suggestions. My thanks to George Sellmer, former college professor and fellow Canal Society of New Jersey member, for gently instructing me in the subtleties of our language. Gratitude also goes to Lucy Fitzgerald, volunteer librarian at the Montclair Historical Society, for helping me with many questions that did not seem to have answers. Both her patience and uncanny ability to find the missing pieces of my puzzle will always be remembered.

The photographs on pp. 16 and 23 appear through the courtesy of Bob Pennisi of Railroad Avenue Enterprises. They helped complete the transportation story. Lastly, I am indebted to the late John Markoe of North Caldwell for sharing his remembrances of a vanished Montclair. John greatly enjoyed looking through my Montclair postcard albums and I savored his recollections while he did so.

My appreciation again to all of you and also to Arcadia for allowing me to share and preserve this "postcard album" that portrays the Montclair of yesteryear.

Introduction

In the early 1900s postcards were an inexpensive yet fairly rapid means of communication. They were also purchased as souvenirs or simply obtained for their own sake as part of the postcard collecting craze in those years. Whether mailed or saved, cards from this era depict the way America looked and lived almost a century ago. In 1913 alone almost one billion cards were sent through the mail. The cards frequently captured images of towns in their most formative years and with the passage of time have become historical documents.

In addition to views of Montclair, many of the postcards in the following chapters have messages written in the margins. These cards generally were mailed before 1907, when it was illegal to write a message on the address side of the card. They make interesting reading.

Montclair has a particularly rich postcard heritage. Over a thousand different cards captured scenes such as a Teddy Roosevelt banner hanging over Bloomfield Avenue during the presidential election year of 1904, carriages waiting at the depot for the midday train to arrive, Montclair Academy's first campus on Bloomfield Avenue, Upper Montclair's business district before its Tudor style predominated, and an architecturally diverse array of homes as they appeared shortly after they were built.

The scenes in the card reappear in the chapters that follow. Although the scenes no longer exist it is hoped that this guide provides an enjoyable and meaningful journey back in time to when they did.

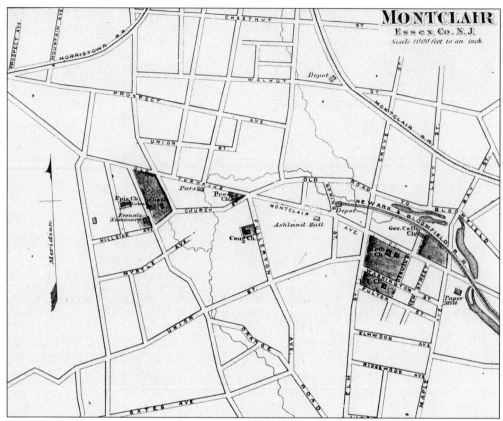

An 1872 map of Montclair.

One

Background

In 1872, Ulysses S. Grant was president and Montclair had been a separate township for only four years. Its 3,000 residents, businesses, and organizations were generally clustered along the Old Turnpike, today's Bloomfield Avenue. The Old Turnpike, chartered in 1806 as the Newark and Pompton Turnpike, originated in Newark and terminated in Parsippany on its western extension and Pompton Plains on its northern branch. By 1872, most of the road's traffic had been lost to the railroads. In that year, Montclair had one railroad that had been in operation for 16 years, a second that was nearing completion, and a third that had just started construction. The map of Montclair on the opposite page shows the streets, major public buildings, and railroads that existed in 1872. Using the map, a walking tour up the Old Turnpike provides background for many of the images of Montclair that appear in later chapters. Also, a brief look at the railroads on the map furnishes an insight into Montclair's future development.

Our tour begins at Montclair's eastern end of the Old Turnpike, where the single-track railroad crossed the street at grade. Just south of the crossing was the Wheeler paper mill, powered by a millpond created by Toney's Brook. A few blocks west of the crossing was the Methodist Episcopal church between Elm Street and Herman Street (today's Hartley Street). Built in 1836, the church was the first building in Montclair to be used solely as a church. As Montclair's population center shifted westward, the church moved to a more central location on North Fullerton Avenue. The last service in the old church was held on December 7, 1879; dedication ceremonies at the new church occurred one week later.

One block south, on Washington Street, stood the Church of the Immaculate Conception, erected around 1856. A new structure was partially completed on North Fullerton Avenue by 1893 and worship services began there in June of that year. The church was finally completed and dedicated in 1909.

Ashland Hall, slightly west of the depot, began as a boarding school in 1845. By 1872 it had become a boarding house with commuters waiting for the two-minute whistle to blow before starting their rush for an east-bound train. Farther up the Old Turnpike, fronting on Valley Road, was one of Montclair's three public schools. Constructed in 1860, the school consisted of primary, grammar, and high school departments.

West of the school, on the corner of Orange Road and Hillside Avenue, was the Hillside Seminary for Young Ladies. The institution was both a day and boarding school and attracted young women from states as distant as California and Florida. Two blocks east, inside the triangle formed by the Old Turnpike, Church Street and Valley Road, stood the Presbyterian church. The church, completed in 1856, closed its doors in 1913 and was razed eight years later. It was replaced by the Hinck Building, which still occupies the site today. West of the church and across from Park Street was the parsonage. It was demolished in the 1920s to allow for the construction of South Park Street. On nearby Fullerton Avenue, construction was progressing on the Congregational church. It would be completed the following year.

Turning to the railroads on the 1872 map, the Newark and Bloomfield Railroad began service to Montclair, then West Bloomfield, in 1856. The line ended at Bloomfield Junction (Roseville Avenue) in Newark, where it connected with the Morris and Essex Railroad. In Montclair, the depot was located just east of Spring Street and slightly north of the Old Turnpike. The depot, the first at this location, was a simple building with a tar-paper roof. It was demolished in 1878.

Lengthy delays at Bloomfield Junction, poor service in general, and high ticket costs were factors behind the creation of a second railroad, the Montclair Railway. The idea originated with Julius Pratt, who became the road's first president. A charter was granted in 1868. The line was to pass through Bloomfield with its eastern terminus at the Pennsylvania Railroad station in Jersey City. Bloomfield's refusal to become bonded for the purpose of constructing a railroad to another town was a major factor in Montclair becoming an independent township in 1868. Service on the line (anticipated by the publishers of the map) began in January of 1873.

The Morristown Railroad, shown in the upper left-hand corner of the map, was actually the Mendham and Chester Railroad, chartered in 1860 to construct a line between Morristown and Mendham. The intent was to extend the line eastward from Morristown to connect with the Montclair Railway north of Chestnut Street. Construction in Montclair began in 1872 at the junction of the two roads and also near Upper Mountain and Claremont Avenues, where a tunnel was to be dug through First Mountain. The Panic of 1873 and the depression which followed stopped work on the road and building was never resumed.

The obstacle posed by First Mountain to transportation in the Montclair area has been significant. The attempt by the Morristown Railroad to penetrate the mountain was both the first and last. In the early 1830s, the Morris Canal circumvented First Mountain by curling around it at Garrett Rock. A few years later the Morris and Essex Railroad ran west to Orange, encountered First Mountain, turned south until it reached Millburn, then resumed its westward journey. A tunnel for Route 280 under First Mountain in the West Orange-Verona area was considered but rejected because of cost. The road was eventually built over the mountain—an option not possible for New Jersey's railroad and canal builders.

Two

Transportation

LACKAWANNA STATION, MONTCLAIR, N. J.

My Dear Elsie — *N.Y. July 20, 190* *I am glad to hear you are having a good time. I will probably write you more at length within the next few days. Mamma said she would write you to-day. Yours, John Giles, Jr.*

In this early 1900s view, the Crawford Building at Bloomfield Avenue and Spring Street is on the left and Lackawanna Station is on the right. The Newark and Bloomfield Railroad was first leased by the Morris and Essex Railroad in 1868; shortly thereafter it was leased to the Delaware, Lackawanna and Western Railroad. The station, the third at this location, existed from 1893 to 1912.

The road between the Crawford Building and the station has had many names over the years. Shortly after the Newark and Pompton Turnpike was built, Israel Crane constructed a road, locally known as the "The Little Turnpike," between his store on the Old Road to Bloomfield (today's Glenridge Avenue) and the new turnpike (now Bloomfield Avenue). The road was officially called Spring Street and the spring in the area was later used to supply water for the steam locomotives serviced at the depot. With the construction of a new and grandiose station in 1913 the name was changed to Lackawanna Plaza. Today it is also known as Israel Crane Way.

Lackawanna Station, Montclair, N. J.

917

The gates in the background are for the Grove Street grade-level crossing. This crossing imposed restrictions on the length of the trains using the depot. To the left of the gates is the water tower used to service steam locomotives, and to the left of the tower is the engine house. Multiple tracks at the right lead to the freight house.

Lackawanna Station, Montclair, N. J.

Because of the expense and difficulty of laying a second track between Toney's Brook and the hillside southeast of Bloomfield Avenue, the railroad was single-tracked. At the left, the rails led to a turntable that positioned the locomotive so it faced east for its return trip to Hoboken. At the right is the freight house.

Lackawanna Station, Montclair, N. J.

435

The station, constructed of brick, was across the street from Mullen's Livery on Bloomfield Avenue. At the western end of the station is a "UNITED STATES EXPRESS" sign, a door reading "BAGGAGE," and a newsstand. Visible at the far right is one of the Lackawanna's passenger coaches.

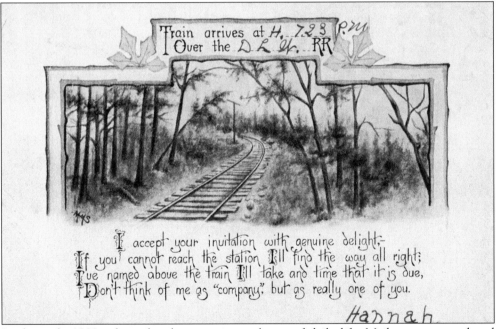

Train arrives at H. 7.23 p.m.
Over the D. L. W. RR.

I accept your invitation with genuine delight;–
If you cannot reach the station I'll find the way all right;
I've named above the train I'll take and time that it is due,
Don't think of me as "company," but as really one of you.

Hannah

In the early 1900s, the railroad was an integral part of daily life. Mail, news, wanted and unwanted relatives—all arrived at the local depot. Rapid mail delivery was possible since intercity trains were frequent; mail was sorted on the train; delivery was twice a day; and, often, the carrier would wait for a response to the card just delivered.

D. L. & W. R. R. PASSENGER TERMINAL.
MONTCLAIR, N. J.

The fourth and last station at this location was designed by William Hull Botsford, an architect for the Delaware, Lackawanna and Western. Botsford perished on the maiden voyage of the *Titanic* in April of 1912. The dedication of the station occurred on June 28, 1913, with Lackawanna president William Truesdale officiating. A town holiday was declared for the occasion and a reception was held at the Hotel Montclair.

The station had six tracks which, until 1945, were used for overnight train storage. Though the station was built for eventual electrification, this card, mailed in 1917, shows it equipped only for steam-powered locomotives. It would not be until September 3, 1930, that an electric train would arrive in Montclair. On that day, the first passenger-carrying electric train run by the railroad left Hoboken with Thomas Edison at the controls and arrived in Montclair with Edison and many railroad dignitaries as passengers.

Service at the station ended February 27, 1981, when the western terminus was relocated to Bay Street. The Lackawanna Station shopping plaza occupies the area today.

The grade-level crossing at the old station limited train length to five passenger cars. With the new station and its longer platforms extending beneath the Grove Street viaduct (pictured above), the maximum number of passenger cars per train was doubled. A second viaduct near Bay Street eliminated the grade-level crossing at Bloomfield Avenue. The building of the latter viaduct was a condition imposed by Montclair on the railroad for receiving permission to build the new terminal. By 1912 the line finally was double-tracked.

The building just east of the Grove Street viaduct housed the steam-powered gristmill of the Harrison Milling Company. Feed, grain, and flour were sold by the company. This was apparently the last of the many paper, cotton, woolen, saw, cider, and gristmills that had operated in Montclair for over two centuries. Depending on their location and needs, the mills used either moving water (Toney's Brook), steam, or animals to power their equipment.

Erie Station, Montclair, N. J.

Within a decade of starting service to Montclair, the Montclair Railway had become the New York and Greenwood Lake Railroad, which was owned by the Erie. Completed in 1873, the station was 13 miles from the railroad's terminus at Jersey City. Just north of the station was a freight house. The railroad was a major factor in developing northern Montclair.

Agitation for a new station began in the early 1900s but it was not until 1926 that a referendum was held, and rejected, on whether to improve the Walnut Street station. Finally, in 1953, after years of declining patronage, a new and smaller station was built on the site of the old freight house. For a brief period in that year the two stations coexisted.

This picture looks just as it does today - a clear cold sky and bare trees - feels just like Thanksgiving!

The original station at Watchung Avenue was on the east side of the single-track railroad. Residential growth in the area was instrumental in its replacement (shown above) being built in 1904. The station name, originally Park Street, was changed to Watchung Avenue after it was suggested that stations named after streets that ran parallel to them was confusing.

This station is at the head of the village street - Will send picture of the village soon. Yours A.

This station, the second at Upper Montclair, was built in 1892. East of the station, visible through the columns, stood the A. Eban Van Gieson residence. The property, today's Erie-Bellevue Plaza, once occupied most of the area between Bellevue and Lorraine Avenues on the west side of Valley Road.

The Upper Montclair station appears today much as it did in the early 1900s. The tower, long gone, pneumatically controlled the gates at Lorraine Avenue while the gates at Bellevue Avenue were mechanically operated by hand. At the right are several freight cars occupying the siding north of Lorraine Avenue, the site of today's small parking lot.

The Mountain Avenue station, built in 1893, is unique among Montclair stations in that it was designed for residential use. Chet and Anna Volski moved into the station in 1935, renovated it, raised their children there, and lived there for over 50 years. Both worked for the Erie Railroad with Anna serving as ticket agent at Mountain Avenue, her home.

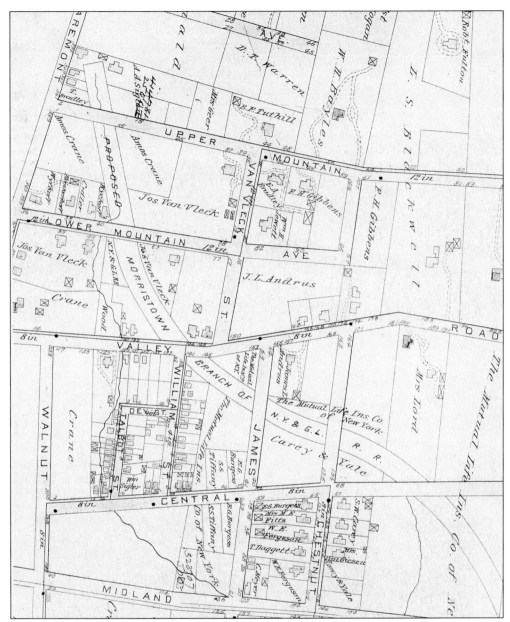

A map of Montclair, 1890. By 1890, charter revisions had changed the proposed Mendham and Chester Railroad to the proposed Morristown Branch of the New York and Greenwood Lake Railroad. Construction of the road began in 1872 but was halted the following year because of financial problems. The western end of the route appears to stop just west of Upper Mountain Avenue but in actuality it was at this point that the railroad would have penetrated First Mountain. The cut leading to the proposed tunnel was visible until 1989 when The Montclair Kimberley Academy filled it in to create the Helmut E. Muenster Field.

Reminders of the construction still exist today and include the embankment east of Central Avenue near Bellaire Drive; the clipped northwest corner of Tierney's on Valley Road adjacent to the right-of-way; and in Verona, the two spits of land on the east and west sides of Verona Lake where abutments were to be placed for a bridge over the lake.

The Centre, Montclair, N. J.

A westbound trolley on Bloomfield Avenue approaches North Fullerton Avenue. In 1896, service between Newark-Glen Ridge and Verona-Caldwell began. The gap was the result of Montclair refusing to grant permission for the laying of rails within its borders. The problem was "solved" using large horse-drawn stagecoaches to transport passengers through Montclair.

Bloomfield Avenue, at Center, Montclair, N. J.

Through service between Newark and Caldwell finally began in 1898 by the North Jersey Street Railway Company, predecessor to Public Service. An eastbound trolley is at Church Street with destination "PENN R.R." In 1927 the line would acquire the route number 29. March 30, 1952, saw the abandonment of the trolley in favor of buses—buses designated number 29.

Valley Road, Montclair, N. J.

The Valley Road line encountered construction problems even more severe than those on the Bloomfield Avenue route. By 1898, construction had been completed from Bloomfield Avenue north to the New York and Greenwood Lake Railroad. The railroad, which then crossed Valley Road at grade, refused to grant permission for trolley rails to be laid across its tracks. In the following year, construction from just north of the railroad to the Passaic County line was completed. Again, horses were used, this time to pull the trolley cars over the railroad so they could continue their journey (the railroad did allow trolley wires to be strung over their right of way). In the summer of 1900 the railroad raised their tracks above street level by building a substantial embankment. This required trolley passengers to scramble up and down the hillside in order to transfer to the waiting trolley on the other side. A few months later a tunnel was cut through the embankment but the missing section of rail was still not installed. Finally, in December, the connection was made and continuous service began. Eventually, a bridge was erected at this location and the road was depressed to compensate for the reduced clearance. The dip in Valley Road near the railroad bridge still bears testimony to the problems of yesterday. The scene above is near Montague Place.

21

Bloomfield Ave., & Valley Road, Montclair, N.J.

Although single-tracked, the Valley Road line had numerous passing sidings to handle north and southbound cars. The trolley is leaving Bloomfield Avenue and turning north onto Valley Road. A switch, manually operated by the motorman, determined the direction of travel at this junction point. The fire headquarters on the right existed from 1904 to 1912.

The new municipal building, at the corner of Valley Road and Bloomfield Avenue, opened in 1913. Closed cars and the elimination of Valley Road trolley service in 1928 date the view as in the mid-1920s. In addition to the north and southbound trolleys, bicycles, automobiles, and a motorcycle round out the transportation scene.

The Montclair trolley barn, at Bloomfield Avenue and Bell Street, opened in 1903 and could accommodate 50 trolley cars. It was used for maintenance and storage of cars from both the Bloomfield Avenue and Valley Road lines. Car 2716 of the Number 29 line, shown entering Bloomfield Avenue, was built for Public Service in 1918. Route numbers, such as 29 for the Bloomfield Avenue line, were used by Public Service beginning in 1927. The Valley Road line, designated Number 59, used that number for less than a year since service was eliminated in January of 1928.

The photograph above was taken shortly before the Bloomfield Avenue line was abandoned on March 30, 1952, in favor of buses. In April, cars were run one at a time from Bell Street down Bloomfield Avenue with a wrecking facility as their eventual destination. Buses never used the trolley barn. The following fall, 35,000 tons of asphalt were laid on top of Bloomfield Avenue to cover the tracks, which, except in a few places, were not removed. Bell Clair Lanes has occupied the building for many years.

Corner of Gates Avenue & Orange Road, Montclair, N.J.

A half century after Montclair saw its first steam locomotive and a decade after it heard the first trolley clang into town, the horse and carriage was still the prevailing mode of private transportation. This view, at the corner of Gates Avenue and Orange Road, is from around 1910. Most of Montclair's streets were unpaved and would remain so until after World War I.

Montclair Center.   Montclair, N. J.

As shown in this 1920s view looking east on Bloomfield Avenue to North Fullerton Avenue, the automobile age has arrived. In the background, the safety island for trolley users created an obstacle for drivers of these gasoline-powered vehicles. The Clairidge Theater, opened in 1922, is advertising "PATHE NEWS FIRST RUN" on its marquee.

24

Three

Business Districts

The Centre, Montclair, N. J.

This is quite a town. look like snow here to-day ~~have~~.

In the fall of 1904, Theodore Roosevelt was the Republican nominee for president with Charles W. Fairbanks as his running mate. The view is looking west on Bloomfield Avenue where Baldwin's Pharmacy had occupied the corner of South Fullerton Avenue and Church Street for the past 30 years and would for the next 20. Standing watch over the centre is the First Presbyterian Church, erected several years before the start of the Civil War. A North Jersey Street Railway Company trolley is traveling east on its journey from Caldwell to Newark. Roosevelt, with strong financial backing, easily defeated Judge Alton B. Parker of New York.

BLOOMFIELD AVE., COR. SPRING ST., MONTCLAIR, N. J.

The Crawford Block, built in 1892, is shown here in the early 1900s. In 1909 John Nolen, an architect, thought it a "fitting type for a country town, and not a small city building in the country." At the extreme right is the Clayton Livery, conveniently located across the street from the unseen railroad depot.

In 1878, the Morris Building was erected at the corner of Bloomfield and Glenridge Avenues. The Montclair Savings Bank, which had opened its door to depositors in 1893 farther west on Bloomfield Avenue, bought the building in 1905. Philip Doremus, whose home was across the street, was the bank's first president. The scene dates from around 1923.

26

MONTCLAIR SAVINGS BANK

The Montclair Savings Bank constructed a new limestone and granite building at the same location in 1924. To the right is the building owned by Edward Madison. Madison's has the distinction of being the first commercial building in Montclair to have an elevator and also the last to have an attended elevator.

The Centre, Montclair, N. J.

916

Across from the Montclair Savings Bank stood the Doremus home on Glenridge Avenue. To the left is the Doremus building, built by Philip Doremus in 1890. Earlier stores on this site were built by Philip in 1853, when Montclair was known as West Bloomfield, and by his father, Peter Doremus, in 1811, when the area was called Cranetown—a different store for each era!

The Doremus store sold groceries, crockery, dry goods, hats, shoes, and hardware. Philip was later joined in the business by his nephew, W. Louis Doremus. Hampton House has occupied the building since 1947. In this c. 1906 view, the Church of the Immaculate Conception is not visible because the church was not completed until 1909.

On North Fullerton Avenue, around the corner from the Doremus store, was Philip Desent's bicycle shop. His neighbor was Dr. Samuel Watkins, Montclair's first dentist, an active citizen and future author. Across the street was Elston M. Harrison's market for meats and vegetables. The presence of the Immaculate Conception tower dates the scene between 1909 and 1914.

The Montclair Trust Company constructed a new limestone building on Bloomfield Avenue in 1914. It was the first of several banks to be built in the next ten years near the "six corners" of Bloomfield Avenue, North and South Fullerton Avenues, Glenridge Avenue, and Church Street.

Dated March 4, 1912, this card carries an advertisement for Montclair Trust Company Travelers' Cheques. At the upper left is the White Star liner *Titanic*. On April 14, 1912, the ship hit an iceberg on her maiden voyage and 1,523 lives were lost. Ironically, the reverse side states the cheques are "the safest, handiest, most satisfactory form of travel funds."

H 2049 Bloomfield Ave., Montclair, N. J.

The above c. 1906 view of Bloomfield Avenue and the one below provide an interesting comparison. Shown are what appears to be a hearse outside the First Presbyterian Church, a pair of eastbound trolleys, and a horse-drawn Montclair Ice wagon turning onto North Fullerton Avenue.

Business Section Bloomfield Ave. Montclair, N. J.

The passing of 20 years has wrought significant change. In 1921, the church was razed and replaced by the Hinck Building. The Spanish Mission-style structure was named for the Hinck family, prominent builders of homes in the Grove-Walnut-Chestnut Street area. The Clairidge Theater marquee is advertising Eleanor Boardman in *The Only Thing*.

At the corner of Bloomfield and South Fullerton Avenues stood the I. Seymour Crane hardware store. Constructed in 1889, the building had a clock with hours designated SEYMOURCRANE. Mr. Crane's interests provided little reason for travel. He was a deacon in the First Presbyterian Church and a director of the Montclair Savings Bank, both across the street.

One block west, on the recently constructed South Park Street, the Montclair Post Office opened for business in a new building in 1925. Hours were from 6:30 in the morning until 7:00 in the evening. The inscription, "U.S. POST OFFICE," can still be read. In 1928 the post office would again relocate, this time farther east on Bloomfield Avenue.

In 1929 the Wedgewood Cafeteria began a long tradition of serving meals in the building previously occupied by the post office. The reverse side of the card reads, "New Jersey's finest cafeteria. Featuring a complete selection of home cooked roasts and seafoods. Children's dinners. Open seven days a week." The Wedgewood closed in 1986.

After its brief stay on South Park Street, the post office moved east to larger headquarters (shown here) on the south side of Bloomfield Avenue. It remained here until 1969, when it moved to its present location on Glenridge Avenue. The Social Security Administration building occupies the former Bloomfield Avenue site today.

Y. M. C. A. Building, Montclair, N.

In 1899 the YMCA opened its new building on the south side of Bloomfield Avenue just west of Park Street. It was founded as "a club that shall offer physical and literary attractions and moral and religious surroundings." It remained at this location for the next 27 years.

New facilities on Park Street were completed in 1926 with Governor A. Harry Moore attending the dedication of the $600,000 building.

Police and Fire Headquarters, Montclair, N. J. Dear Clara. 1/20/06

If nothing happens I will come home. Wednesday the 24th this month. Barbara.

The brick and stone building at the northeast corner of Bloomfield Avenue and Valley Road was constructed in 1904 to be used as headquarters for the police and fire departments. At that time, the Montclair Fire Department was still a volunteer organization consisting of approximately 100 men at four different locations.

Municipal Building, Montclair, N. J.

After extensive remodeling of the old structure (including a totally new facade), the new Municipal Building opened in 1913. It housed not only the fire and police departments but local government offices as well. By the next year, the volunteer system was totally eliminated and all fire-fighting personnel were on a fully paid basis.

BLOOMFIELD AVE. & VALLEY ROAD, MONTCLAIR, N. J.

Dear Sigrid: We are in New Jersey and are hav a lovely time there are some beautifull places are here. That car where you see the mark passes right by the ho a. s. s.

The Borden's Condensed Milk Company was located on the northwest corner of Bloomfield Avenue and Valley Road at the time this c. 1904 photograph was taken. Farther up the avenue was the car barn of the North Jersey Street Railway Company used by both Bloomfield Avenue and Valley Road trolleys. One of them has just entered Bloomfield Avenue from the barn.

PUBLIC SERVICE BUILDING, MONTCLAIR, N. J.

The Public Service building, on the corner of Bloomfield Avenue and Bell Street, occupies center stage in this early 1920s view. In the left window is presumably the latest model in gas stoves. The triangular logo on the sign represents the gas, electric, and transportation services provided by the company. At the right is the Public Service trolley barn.

The limestone and brick building on the southwest corner of Valley Road and Bellevue Avenue was constructed around 1910. Later used by the Montclair Trust Company, the bank's name is still discernible at the top of the building. On the other side of Bellevue Avenue stood the Park Side Pharmacy, the first building in Upper Montclair to have electric lights.

This early 1900s view looks west from Bellevue Avenue toward Valley Road. An advertisement for the Park Side Pharmacy reads, "POPULAR PRICE DRUG STORE ALWAYS UP TO DATE PRESCRIPTIONS OUR SPECIALTY." In the summer, tables and chairs were set up on a large outdoor platform where ice cream was served. The building survived until 1915.

Belleville Avenue, Upper Montclair, N. J.

Seen from the Erie crossing, the buildings on the left were located at today's Erie-Bellevue Plaza. To the right of Philip Young's bicycle shop was the Cliffside (in the late 1800s the name of Upper Montclair) Livery Stable. Partly visible across the street is the Trunk Building (named for its shape), which was later replaced by the Bellevue Theater.

UPPER MONTCLAIR CENTER

By the early 1920s the south side of Bellevue Avenue had dramatically changed. The post office and theater were constructed in a Tudor style at the suggestion of Robert Anderson, a member of the family for whom the park was named. At the Bellevue Theater, *The Perfect Flapper* is playing.

Highgate Hall occupied the second floor of the Bellevue Theater building. The reverse side of the card reads, "Having a party or an anniversary? We will reserve a table for a dinner party of four or more and without extra charge will furnish a cake for the occasion."

FIRST NATIONAL BANK, Upper Montclair, N. J.

PUB. BY LEMBERT & LEVINE

In 1915, the Montclair National Bank and Trust Company began business at the northwest corner of Valley Road and Bellevue Avenue. The building occupied the site previously used by the Park Side Pharmacy. To the left of the clock, a sign reading "GO SLOW" was placed at the center of the intersection when the traffic officer was on duty.

J.B. Fox and Company, sellers of stationery and dry goods, stood at the northeast corner of Valley Road and Bellevue Avenue around 1908. A lavishly outfitted wagon (pulled by a team of horses) and the parked open touring car contrast the past and future of vehicular travel in Upper Montclair.

VALLEY ROAD SHOWING MASONIC TEMPLE BUILDING.   UPPER MONTCLAIR, N. J.

The Masonic Temple building, located at the corner of Valley Road and Lorraine Avenue, was constructed in 1920. Since its founding in 1949, the Olympic Shop has occupied the building. The shop was named for the 1940 Olympic Games aspirations of its owner—games never held in that pre-war year. The trolley wires would be removed after the cessation of service in 1928.

THE FIRST NATIONAL BANK OF MONTCLAIR AT THE B[

This view of Bellevue Avenue and the one below of Valley Road are from one postcard.

BUSINESS CENTER.   UPPER MONTCLAIR, N. J.

This card evokes feelings of a quiet, warm, summer day—perhaps a Wednesday afternoon when many stores were closed. By 1930 the trolley was gone and the business district of Upper Montclair had essentially attained its present-day appearance.

Four
Education

Public School, Montclair, N. J.

This view of the Central Grammar and Central Primary Schools, looking northwest from the corner of Valley Road and Church Street, was taken around 1904. The sender was kind enough to symbolically identify the buildings. The grammar school was actually comprised of three different sections: the first and northwest section was built in 1860, the southwest wing in 1869, and the eastern portion (including the belfry) in 1873. West of the grammar school was the primary school; the western half was built in 1878–79 while the eastern half (replete with octagonal cupola and weathervane) was built in 1884. Behind the two schools stood the shop building, which housed classrooms for cooking and clay modeling. In the background, fronting on Orange Road, was the high school, which opened for classes in 1893.

OLD GRAMMAR SCHOOL
MONTCLAIR, N. J.

The grammar school has been used for various functions over the years. At the start of the Civil War, a regiment of the Essex Brigade used it for drilling purposes. In 1866, when the war was over, a high school curriculum was introduced. In 1909 the building was converted into administrative offices for the school system. The belfry was removed in 1924.

Montclair Public School, Montclair, N.J.

In 1874, Randall Spaulding became principal of the high school, and shortly thereafter he became the superintendent of schools. Among his many innovations was the introduction of manual training into the curriculum, and the primary school (above) was remodeled for that purpose. The former school is now used for administrative functions.

Montclair's first high school building opened on Orange Road on September 16, 1893. Its many features included several foot warmers on the first floor for drying both the feet and clothing of students, chemistry and photography laboratories, a second-floor auditorium with a capacity of 500, and a room on the third floor for use as a gymnasium.

This scene was photographed from the high school tower. At the lower left is the rear of the former St. Luke's Episcopal Church, built in 1870. Twenty years later, the church moved to South Fullerton Avenue and the property was sold to the board of education. The former church was then converted into a gymnasium for use by the high school.

In the center of the card is an iron flagstaff. The high school itself was situated so that natural light would come over the left shoulder and back of each student in the classrooms on the south side of the building (shown above). On the north side were recitation rooms, a reference room, the library, and the principal's office with a fireplace.

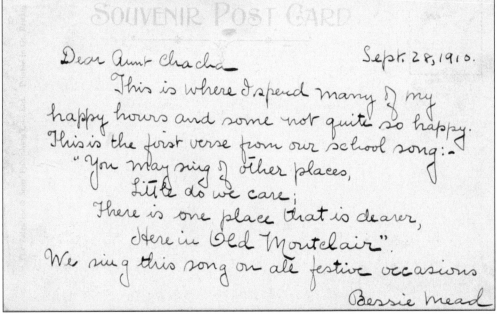

The message side of the postcard at the top of the page is shown above. Bessie Mead certainly expressed herself both legibly and well. She was presumably the daughter of Reverend Charles Mead, who resided at 199 Walnut Street. According to a Montclair Directory from 1904–1905, this was the only Mead family in town.

44

The Hillside Grammar School was built at the corner of Orange Road and Hillside Avenue in 1909 and occupied the site previously used by the Hillside Seminary for Young Ladies. In 1910, its student population of 707 was larger than that of any other Montclair school. The high school is visible at the right.

The high school occupied its Orange Road building until 1915, when the current high school on Chestnut Street opened. In that year, the old high school, converted to an elementary school, was renamed Spaulding School in honor of the former superintendent. Mr. Spaulding had retired in 1912 after 38 years of service. The school was razed in the mid-1930s.

From 1894 to 1900 the student population in the Montclair Public Schools increased from 1,600 to 2,700. To partially meet this increased demand, the Maple Avenue School was erected in 1896, a short distance south of Bloomfield Avenue, to replace the Washington School. Twenty years later its name was changed to the Glenfield School.

An increased demand for school facilities was felt in all sections of Montclair. The 200-by-200-foot Watchung School on North Fullerton Avenue between Frederick and Garden Streets was completed in 1900. The property and school, consisting of two furnished and two unfurnished classrooms, cost $12,000.

Education in Upper Montclair initially consisted of a Sabbath School conducted in an 1816 barn. Around 1827, the first Mount Hebron School was constructed on the corner of Valley Road and Bellevue Avenue. The second school, at Bellevue and Norwood Avenues, was erected in 1884. In 1893, the third school (shown here) was built on its predecessor's foundation.

The fourth Mount Hebron school (above) was completed in 1909 at the southeast corner of Lorraine and Norwood Avenues. Three additional units would be constructed over the next two decades, with the last addition requiring the razing of the 1893 school. A 1972 renovation gave the school its current appearance.

47

BIRD'S-EYE VIEW OF SCHOOL BUILDING

Hope to see you soon   *Viola*

In 1887, at the age of 27, John George MacVicar was employed to teach college-bound boys of local families. His school, the Montclair School for Boys, soon called Montclair Academy, consisted of 18 students in a one-room building on Clinton Avenue. At the end of the school year enrollment had almost doubled and a new location was sought. By September, several acres near the western end of Montclair just south of Bloomfield Avenue had been purchased and a Recitation Hall had been built. The bird's-eye view above portrays the campus as it appeared in 1906. Bloomfield Avenue is at the right and Walden Place is at the bottom of the card.

At the top of the card, fronting on Lloyd Place (later Road), is Bradley House, which was built in 1896. The building, a dormitory with luxurious accommodations for 30 students, also provided living quarters for George MacVicar and his wife, Harriet. At the left is Walden House, a dormitory. To the right of Walden House and facing Walden Place is the Recitation Building; to its rear is the Gymnasium Building. The one-and-one-half-story structure just north of the gymnasium is the swimming pool, which was completed in 1906.

Military Academy, Montclair, N. J.

The Recitation Building, the first building on the new campus, is in the foreground. As a cost-cutting move, Headmaster MacVicar constructed the building's foundation himself. The gymnasium, built in the early 1890s, is at the rear of the Recitation Building. It would house athletic events into the 1960s.

Bradley Hall, Military Academy, Montclair, N. J.

In the early 1890s, a boarding house for students was maintained in an old home on the north side of Bloomfield Avenue across from the school. MacVicar's exasperation with constant maintenance and a substantial loan from Edwin A. Bradley, the president of a building materials company, were the major factors behind the construction of Bradley House.

Hoisting Old Glory, Military Academy, Montclair, N. J.

How would you like to be here, The soldiers all march around, the Academy every evening. Montclair is a magnificent country place wish you were here Good bye M. H

As a means to increase enrollment, the school instituted a military program in 1891 and correspondingly changed its name to the Montclair Military Academy. In August 1906, the sender of this card wrote: "How would you like to be here? The soldiers all march around the Academy every evening. Montclair is a magnificent country place wish you were here. Good bye: M. H."

EXIBITION DRILL, 1905, M. M. A.

Drill was part of the regimen at the Montclair Military Academy for 18 years. In 1909, Headmaster MacVicar dropped the military program and the school became Montclair Academy. This 1905 scene shows Old Glory with 45 stars; Oklahoma, New Mexico, Arizona, Alaska, and Hawaii had not yet joined the Union. The residences are north of Bradley House.

Firing Line, Military Academy, Montclair, N. J.   75

September 24th 1909.
6 Lloyd Road -   *Your friend,*
Montclair N.J. -   *E. L. B.*

Each school year's military culmination was a mock battle held in May on the drill field, today's athletic field. The annual event was witnessed by many residents from the vantage point of the hillside. E.L.B., the sender of this card, was Emma Blauvelt, a widow, who resided at 6 Lloyd Road (the house shown in the upper left-hand corner of the card).

Montclair Military Academy
Montclair, N. J.

As a result of increased enrollment, the Recitation Building became inadequate by the early 1900s. Again, Edwin Bradley assisted by assuming all of MacVicar's debts in the form of a $100,000 loan. The loan provided the means to raze the Recitation Building and erect the above Academic Building ("Acky") in its place in 1909. Acky lasted until 1964.

51

Ashland Hall, located on the south side of Bloomfield Avenue slightly west of the depot, was a boarding school for boys in the mid-1800s. By the early 1870s it had become a boarding house for commuters who waited for the two-minute whistle to blow before beginning their sprint for an eastbound train. Ashland Hall survived until the early twentieth century.

Cloverside School, Montclair, N. J.

V 276

During the Civil War, Lewis St. John Benedict purchased 12 acres and a residence on the southeast corner of Mountain (now South Mountain) and Bloomfield Avenues. In 1903, Seelye, his son, sold the property to Elizabeth Timlow, an educator. For the next six years, the residence housed the Cloverside School for Girls with Ms. Timlow as principal.

The Montclair Art Museum opened in January of 1914 on the former property of the Cloverside School for Girls. The museum came into being when William T. Evans donated 54 American paintings contingent on their being housed in a fire-proof structure. Florence Rand Lang's donation of $50,000 provided for the suitable structure.

1 EXTERIOR
MONTCLAIR ART MUSEUM, MONTCLAIR, NEW JERSEY

By the end of 1931, the museum had essentially attained its present-day appearance. In 1924, the front facade was improved by the addition of a pair of marble columns on each side of the entrance. Seven years later, an east wing was added which provided increased display area on the main floor and classrooms below. Again, Florence Rand Lang assisted.

In 1878, seven years after immigrating to the United States from Austria, Joseph Francis Mendl became rector of the Church of the Immaculate Conception. Father Mendl soon established a parochial school in Tegakwita Hall at the corner of Munn Street and Cottage Place. The building was named for a Native American girl who was persecuted for her beliefs.

The above structure, at the corner of Park Street and Lorraine Avenue, was built in 1894 for Dr. Morgan W. Ayres. In 1920 the residence was bought by the Dominican Sisters of Caldwell and named, simply, Lacordaire. The message on the card, mailed September 8, 1930, reads in part, "Our school opens on the 15th. God bless you all and send success for coming year—Lovingly, Sr. Aurelia."

State Normal School, Montclair Heights, N. J.

College Hall is seen here during the final stages of construction. The school, then New Jersey State Normal School, offered a two-year program for teachers. Governor John Franklin Fort was present at the 1908 dedication. In 1927 the school became Montclair State Teachers' College, which featured a four-year program for secondary teachers.

New Jersey State Normal School, Montclair N. J.

Gretta Dobbins mailed this card in 1911 and wrote, "Sometime when you are studying hard just think of me in the building studying or running down the board walk for a trolley car." The trolley was the Valley Road trolley which ended its run at Normal Avenue. In 1958 the school became Montclair State College. It is now Montclair State University.

The Munn House, near the corner of Church Street and Valley Road, was opened as a public house around 1807. The 12-room building later became a residence and in the late 1890s was modified for use as the Free Public Library. It was later moved to the rear of its property and exists today as part of the Evangelical Covenant Church.

In 1901, the Andrew Carnegie Foundation donated $40,000 to the town for a new library. The library was constructed at the corner of Church Street and Valley Road near the former site of the Munn House. This "New Year's card" was published by Madison's, today Montclair's oldest business.

The new library opened its doors on April 14, 1904, and remained at this corner location until 1955. Many of Mr. Carnegie's architectural suggestions, such as a short flight of stairs leading to a central entrance, were incorporated into its design. Currently, the former library is owned by and physically connected to the Unitarian church.

By the late 1940s, the storage capacity and service areas of the Carnegie Library were no longer adequate. Largely through the generosity of the Davella Mills Foundation, construction of a new library on South Fullerton Avenue was completed in 1955. The late 1990s again witnessed movement of the library, an expansion both outward—and upward!

PUBLIC LIBRARY, UPPER MONTCLAIR, N. J.

The Bellevue Avenue Branch of the Montclair Public Library, designed by architect Francis Augustus Nelson, opened its doors in 1914. Nelson also designed the Upper Montclair Women's Club and the Upper Montclair Post Office. Again, the construction of the library was financed by a donation from the Carnegie Foundation. Montclair's libraries were two of the more than 1,600 endowed by Carnegie at a cost of 43 million dollars. This philanthropy was certainly in keeping with his philosophy that, "The man who dies rich, dies disgraced." A portrait of Mr. Carnegie rests on a wall near the main desk in the Bellevue Avenue Branch. Above the entrance to the library is the following inscription: "HE THAT LOVETH A BOOK WILL NEVER WANT A FAITHFUL FRIEND, A WHOLESOME COUNSELLOR, A CHEERFUL COMPANION, AN EFFECTUAL COMFORTER."

Five
Churches

PRESBYTERIAN CHURCH, MONTCLAIR, N. J.

From 1838 until 1856, the West Bloomfield Presbyterian Society used a remodeled school building for its worship services. The converted school was located at the corner of Bloomfield Avenue and what would later become Church Street. In 1856 a new Presbyterian church was erected at the same location. The church, enclosed by an iron fence, was constructed of brownstone from local quarries. Its steeple, originally pointed, was later struck during an electrical storm and was capped rather than repaired. After the founding of other Presbyterian churches in Montclair toward the end of the century, the church became the First Presbyterian Church and was affectionately known as "Old First." The above scene is of the church with its chapel to the rear shortly after the turn of the century.

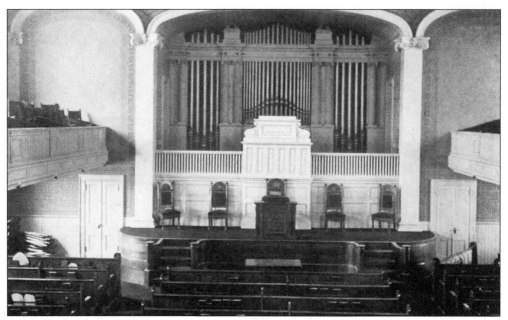

The interior of the Presbyterian church is shown as it appeared sometime after 1870. In 1913 the church closed its doors and it was demolished eight years later, its brownstone carted away for other purposes. The Hinck Building was constructed on the site in 1921.

1776.   1876.

CENTENNIAL CELEBRATION

MONTCLAIR. N. J.

July Fourth, 1876.

The Presbyterian church was the center of Montclair's Centennial Celebration on July 4, 1876. Revolutionary war relics were displayed including a pair of shoe buckles worn in mourning for the death of George Washington. Exercises inside the church began at 10 a.m. with Montclair's clergy and older citizens seated on a platform at the front of the church. At 9:30 that evening, barrels of tar that had been placed on the hillside were set afire to provide a fitting and emotional end to the celebration. The cover page of the program for the centennial celebration is shown at the left.

TRINITY PRESBYTERIAN CHURCH MONTCLAIR, N.J.

Dedication, Oct. 15, 1905

Trinity Presbyterian Church had its roots in Old First. The church held its first worship service in rented quarters on October 17, 1886, and its first baptism took place eight weeks later. Annie Yarrington Watkins, the daughter of Samuel Watkins and the granddaughter of Philip Doremus, was baptized that Sunday morning. By the following spring a chapel had been built near the corner of Church Street and Valley Road, one block from the church's origins. Within a decade the congregation had outgrown the building and soon purchased land on the northwest corner of Midland and Claremont Avenues. The new church, shown above, was dedicated on October 15, 1905. Eight years later, on December 2, 1913, Trinity and Old First merged to form Central Presbyterian Church. At month's end, Old First closed its doors and the merged congregations began worshiping together in the former Trinity Church sanctuary. In 1922 a new Central Presbyterian Church on the corner of Park Street and Claremont Avenue was dedicated. The following year Trinity Church was razed.

SOUTH FULLERTON AVENUE, SHOWING CONGREGATIONAL CHURCH, MONTLA...

The Congregational church was organized in January of 1870 with many of its charter members coming from Old First. Services were initially held on the third floor of the Pillsbury Building, a frame structure that preceded the I. Seymour Crane Hardware Store on the corner of Bloomfield and South Fullerton Avenues. In June of that year a call was extended to Amory Howe Bradford and in September Reverend Bradford was ordained and installed. Within a few months Pillsbury Hall was no longer adequate and a site for a new church was selected on Fullerton Avenue (later designated South Fullerton after the building of North Fullerton Avenue). On October 15, 1873, the church, pictured above, was dedicated. ¹   ⁻ leading the church for over 40 years, Reverend Bradford died and a day of   ...⸰ observed by the town. Three years later, on March 20, 1914, the church was totally   ⸰yed in a fire. For the next two years the congregation used Old First for their services—a scant three months after Old First had been vacated. During this period the building of the current church was undertaken.

62

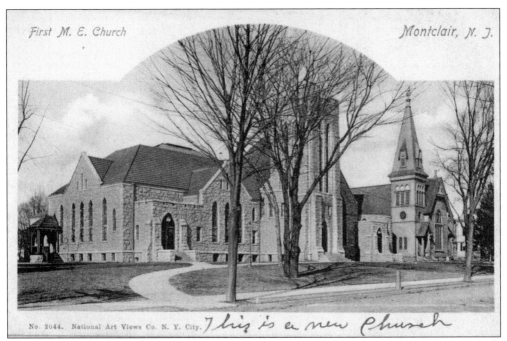

First M. E. Church   Montclair, N. J.

No. 2044. National Art Views Co. N. Y. City. *This is a new church*

The Methodist Episcopal Society of West Bloomfield was organized in 1836 and built Montclair's first church on the Old Turnpike near Elm Street. In 1879 the society moved to a larger church on North Fullerton Avenue. By 1902, a large stone church had been built just south of the old church. As shown, both churches coexisted for a short time.

The first Church of the Immaculate Conception was erected around 1856 on Washington Street near Elm Street. In 1893, the cornerstone for a new structure on North Fullerton Avenue was put in place. One year later, because of financial and structural problems, construction was halted and a roof put over the basement so services could be held. In 1909, bell chimes were placed in the tower of the completed church, shown at right, and the structure was dedicated on September 26 of that same year.

63

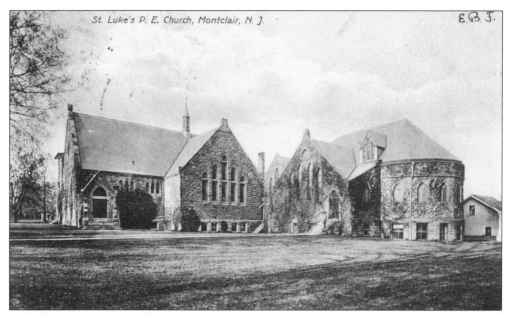

St. Luke's P. E. Church, Montclair, N. J.   E.G.J.

St. Luke's Parish, organized in 1860, initially met in a frame building at Montclair's eastern end of the turnpike. A decade later a new church was completed on St. Luke's Place (p. 43). In the late 1880s construction began for a larger church on South Fullerton Avenue. The first service in the new edifice, to the left in the above photograph, was in 1890.

First Baptist Church Montclair, N. J.

The First Baptist Church, on South Fullerton Avenue near Bloomfield Avenue, held its first service in 1891. Two decades later the church moved to a significantly larger structure on Church Street. At that time the South Fullerton Avenue building began serving the needs of the First Church of Christ, Scientist. It is now a Masonic Lodge.

The first services in the new Baptist church were held in 1911. Its pastor, Dr. Harry Emerson Fosdick, led the congregation from 1904 until 1915 and occupied the pulpit in both churches. Dr. Fosdick's renown has given him a place in Webster's biographical section for many years. The sign for the Carnegie Free Public Library appears at the lower left.

UNITARIAN CHURCH, MONTCLAIR, N. J.

The Unitarian Church, the successor to the Unitarian Society, was organized in 1897. After meeting in a private residence, the congregation moved into its new home, shown above, in 1905. The former Carnegie Library is now owned by and physically connected to the church. At the far left is the rear of the Swedish Congregational Church, which faced Valley Road.

In 1890 Grace Presbyterian Church held its first worship service in the Erie station on Walnut Street. One year later a new church was built at Forest and Chestnut Streets. The last move, to the corner of Grove Street and Tuxedo Road, was in 1926. Based on the building material to the left and the church's appearance, this photograph was probably taken that year.

The Watchung Avenue Congregational Church was dedicated in 1905. Eleven years later the Community House was constructed. Used by both church and town, it had Montclair's largest stage when built. The church was destroyed by fire in 1974 and was never rebuilt. Today, the Montclair Community Church has its home in the 1916 structure.

66

Old Congregational Church, Upper Montclair, N. J.

The Christian Union Congregational Church, located on Valley Road south of Cooper Avenue, held its first worship service in April of 1882. A log cabin used by General Lafayette had occupied the site during the Revolutionary War. A stone used as a doorstep to the cabin is the focus of a memorial park at this location today.

C. U. CONGREGATIONAL CHURCH, MONTCLAIR N. J.

Moderation is the silken string running through the pearl-chain of all virtues. Remember this on the 7th.

ALBERT WRENSCH, MONTCLAIR. N. J.

Cooper Avenue was named for Mary and Harriet Cooper, sisters who lived on property that extended from Valley Road to Northview Avenue, just north of the church shown at the top of the page. The present church, above, dedicated in 1900, is on Cooper Avenue west of Park Street. It was erected on the site of an orchard and farm given by the sisters to the church.

St. James Episcopal Church. Upper Montclair, N. J.

The Cliffside Chapel, the first church in Upper Montclair, was completed in 1878 on the southeast corner of Valley Road and Bellevue Avenue. Dedicated as a Presbyterian church, the structure was sold in 1885 to Episcopalians for use as a mission of St. Luke's Church. Three years later the Parish of Saint James was established.

ST. JAMES EPISCOPAL CHURCH, Upper Montclair, N. J.

PUB. BY LÉMBERT & LEVINE

In 1919, the year after the end of World War I, a new bell tower was built both as a memorial to those who died in the war and as an expression of gratitude for those who returned safely. Within the tower were placed eleven bronze bells, seven of which were inscribed with the names of servicemen killed in the war.

The Upper Montclair Presbyterian Church, situated in a picturesque, semi-circular area formed by Norwood, Inwood, and Fernwood Avenues, laid the cornerstone for its new chapel in 1907. The chapel, shown from Norwood Avenue, was made of small blocks of traprock obtained from the nearby Osborne and Marsellis quarry (p. 118).

In 1911 ground was broken for a larger church building, just south of the chapel. The granite edifice was the gift, as was the land, chapel, and manse before it, of Timothy and Caroline Sellew. In 1925 a parish house and Sunday school were built around the chapel, which then became the auditorium for the enlarged structure.

In the mid-1800s, Speertown, the northern part of today's Montclair, contained less than 30 dwellings. One of them, still existing on Upper Mountain Avenue just over the border in Little Falls, was the home of Peter G. Speer. It was here that Thomas Van Reyper from Stone House Plains, the northern part of today's Bloomfield, courted Peter's daughter Caroline. After marriage and children, the family moved into their new home on Valley Road opposite Mount Hebron Cemetery around 1872. Their house, now the Van Reyper/Bond house, is today part of Montclair State University.

In 1892, a group of Speertown residents met at the Van Reyper home for a worship service and discussion of forming a church in northern Montclair. Five years later the Montclair Heights Reformed Church was officially organized and construction soon began on a permanent home. In 1901, on a plot of land donated by the heirs of Peter G. Speer, the new church was dedicated. Many decades later, in a nostalgic skit at the church, reference was made to the fence which had once enclosed both the church (above) and its neighbor, Mount Hebron Cemetery. It was said, "Naturally, potential church members hesitated about joining up, since they were not sure whether they were attending a church service or going to their own funeral."

Six
Lodging and Leisure

The Montclair (later known as the Hotel Montclair), situated at the top of First Mountain slightly north of Bloomfield Avenue, opened its doors for guests on May 1, 1907. In those overlapping years of the carriage era and the automobile age, the hotel provided shelter for both. Golf privileges were to be enjoyed at the Montclair Golf Club, a short distance south of the hotel on Mount Prospect Avenue in Verona.

OPEN THE ENTIRE YEAR   HOTEL MONTCLAIR   MONTCLAIR, N. J.

Located on the mountain crest, the hostelry appropriately faced Crestmont Road. One of the forces in establishing the hotel was Paul Wilcox of Upper Mountain Avenue. A lawyer, Wilcox was an early proponent of the Bank of Montclair, a major figure in the formative years of both the Montclair Golf Club and Hotel Montclair, and, later in life, manager of the hotel.

LOOKING TO BLOOMFIELD AVENUE FROM CRESTMONT ROAD, MONTCLAIR, N. J.

This view is east from the corner of Claremont Avenue and Crestmont Road. At the left, a pedestrian entrance to the hotel is marked by a sign reading "HOTEL MONTCLAIR." The entrance was convenient for those guests arriving by trolley.

Hotel Montclair, Montclair, N. J.

July 22ⁿᵈ / 907.

This card shows the hotel in its final stages of construction. Although dated July 22, 1907, less than three months after the facility opened, the unfinished grounds and the presence of building material suggest the photograph was taken before the hotel opened its doors to guests. The message on the card reads, "This is 'the' hotel. It is a beauty."

SOLARIUM　　HOTEL MONTCLAIR – Montclair, N. J.　　FREDERICK C. HALL, PRESIDENT

Designed for socializing and relaxation, the solarium had a western exposure and was adjacent to the main entrance. By the mid-1930s the hotel would also feature an English grill and taproom. The repeal of Prohibition in 1933 made the latter possible. Panoramic views, wide lawns, and artesian wells were other attractions.

73

The lounge was undoubtedly a bit more active on June 28, 1913, than in the view above. On that day the fourth and last Delaware, Lackawanna and Western Railroad station was dedicated and a town holiday was declared. Commemorating the occasion, speeches were given and a luncheon was served—at the Hotel Montclair.

After serving guests for a third of a century, the hotel was razed and replaced by the Rockcliffe Apartments. In 1940 Mayor Speers set in place the new cornerstone containing copies of the *Montclair Times*, *New York Times*, and the plans for Rockcliffe. Murals with historical scenes created for Rockcliffe now grace the walls of the Israel Crane House.

Montclair, N. J. Mountain House, Bloomfield Ave.

Built in the 1830s, the front half of the above structure was on the western end of Claremont Avenue south of the Hotel Montclair. It originally housed the Mount Prospect Institute, a school for young men and women. In the 1870s, many years after the school had closed, the building was renovated and became the Mountain House, a residence for boarders.

Mountain House, Montclair, N. J.

Within a few years the Mountain House had become popular enough to warrant an addition to its western side. After the introduction of trolley service, its boarders could travel via the "Mountain House Special" between their residence and the Delaware, Lackawanna and Western station. The Dorchester Condominiums occupy the site today.

The Inn, Malboro Park, Montclair, N. J.

The Inn, built in 1867 at the corner of Watchung Avenue and Grove Street, was initially the residence of Samuel Holmes, who named it and the surrounding 17 acres "Holmeswood." After Holmes' death in 1897, the building was remodeled and in 1903 opened as the Marlboro Inn. Real estate owned by Holmes in this area was developed as Marlboro Park.

In the 1920s the inn received a Tudor-style addition on its eastern side. Part of the original structure, containing kitchen and dining facilities, is visible at the left of the card. Many celebrities, including Helen Hayes, Bette Davis, and former New Jersey Governor Brendan Byrne, have been guests at the Marlboro Inn over the years.

The Mansion House, on the southeast corner of Bloomfield Avenue and Valley Road, was originally built by Joseph Munn as the West Bloomfield Hotel. Later sold to Edward Wright, it was remodeled in the late 1800s and renamed the Mansion House. Signs inform the public of pleasures within—a cafe, Feigenspan beer, the hotel—something for everyone!

MONTCLAIR THEATRE, MONTCLAIR, N. J.

After the Mansion House was razed, the Montclair Theater was built on the site and opened in 1913. It was the first of the town's theaters and offered concerts, vaudeville, plays, lectures, silent movies, and later talkies. Its asbestos stage curtain portrayed a 1913 scene of Bloomfield Avenue. A municipal parking lot has occupied the area for decades.

The Montclair Club, located on the southern side of Church Street near its eastern end, opened its doors in 1889 to a throng of 1,200. Conveniently, carriages (and later, cars) using the porte cochere on the left could leave the grounds by using an exit on The Crescent. Seelye Benedict, whose home was where the Montclair Art Museum is now, was a major force behind the club's creation. Designed for recreation and socializing, it featured bowling alleys in the basement and billiard, pool, reading, and card rooms on the first floor. A 500-seat music hall, dressing rooms, and parlors occupied the second floor while the uppermost level contained a dining room, kitchen, and living quarters. Gambling and alcohol were not allowed. Competition from other organizations eventually eroded its membership base and the club was disbanded with a farewell dinner on May 24, 1924. The structure was soon razed and in 1930 the building that currently occupies the site was constructed on the club's expansive front lawn. A municipal parking lot now occupies the former site of the clubhouse.

The Montclair Athletic Club was formed in 1891 with George Inness Jr. as its first president. Seven acres of land between Valley Road and Central Avenue were soon bought and activities officially began in 1893. The clubhouse above was used as both lounge and meeting place. At the far left is the grandstand.

Starting in the 1930s, The Kimberley School and Montclair Academy began using the above athletic field. Because of dwindling club membership, the property was sold to The Kimberley School in 1949 and is today The Montclair Kimberley Academy Middle School. Club Street, across Valley Road, serves as a reminder of the area's past.

MONTCLAIR, N. J.   The Mountain Slope from Erwin Park.

[handwritten postcard message] *Home again. Start in on Monday. Will write later. Montclair's very pretty spots. Emma.*

The Montclair Golf Club was organized in 1893 and the following year built a nine-hole golf course between Central Avenue and Park Street north of Chestnut Street. The course had both expected and unexpected hazards. First, the Erie Railroad embankment, built in 1873 but never used (p. 19), was a substantial and frustrating obstacle. Second, within two years, new home construction in the Erwin Park area signaled a short future for the course's leased grounds. The solution was close at hand. Adequate acreage west of Valley Road, roughly in the area of today's Edgemont Park, was available for lease. In the spring of 1896 the new course was ready for use. A portion of the course, looking west to North Mountain Avenue, is shown above. The log clubhouse was just west of Valley Road and slightly north of its intersection with Central Avenue.

Irwin Golf Club Course, Montclair, N. J.

V 216

Within two years, problems arose. Increased membership made the course cramped and home building encroached upon it. In 1898 the club began purchasing large parcels of land in Verona and the first nine holes were playable the following year. The Valley Road course above then passed into the hands of the Erwin Park Golf Club for a number of years.

Montclair Golf Links Montclair N. J.

Bounded on the east by Mount Prospect Avenue and on the north by Sunset Avenue, the new course in Verona had been in use for about a dozen years when this photograph was taken. The view, looking northeast toward Bloomfield Avenue, captured the Hotel Montclair several years after it was built. The hotel's "golf privileges" were quite convenient.

GOLF CLUB HOUSE, MONTCLAIR, N. J.

This scene, actually in Verona, is looking north from the rear of the clubhouse located just west of Mount Prospect Avenue. By late spring of 1900 the clubhouse was ready for use, and on May 19 President Paul Wilcox and the membership celebrated its completion. The following spring the full complement of 18 holes were available for play.

Montclair Golf Club, Montclair, N. J.

By late 1905 the original clubhouse had been expanded to accommodate an increased membership. The north side, with its wide porch facing the course, appears of greater height because of the sharply sloped terrain. On October 3, 1922, the building was totally destroyed by fire. The current clubhouse, enlarged over the years, is its successor.

82

In 1922, the Wellmont, Clairidge, and Bellevue theaters opened their doors. In this era before sound tracks, all three were built for live stage shows, plays, and silent movies. Musical accompaniment was provided by an organ; the Wellmont's came from the Montclair Theater. *Marriage License* was being featured at the Wellmont.

In this mid-1920s scene, neither people nor signs nor lights were needed to control traffic at Bloomfield Avenue and Church Street. The corner facade of the Hinck Building had not yet been altered and the Clairidge boasted marquees on both streets. A Borden Milk Company wagon is parked near the Church Street entrance to the building.

Montclair Theatre, Montclair, N. J.

P-26133 (B)

The Montclair Theater was razed in the early 1950s with much of the building bulldozed into its basement in the process. Over time, the settling and rotting of the material was responsible for the sinking of the municipal parking lot built on the site. Briefly, the remains of the theater were visible during the reconstruction of the lot in 1997.

Bellevue Theatre,   Upper Montclair, N. J.

In its early years the Bellevue Theater entrance sported a canopy rather than a marquee. With the reconstruction of the theater in 1997, its overly protruding marquee, oft hit by a bus leaving Erie-Bellevue Plaza, was replaced. As part of the renovation, the retail space at the right of the building became the concession area for the remodeled theater.

84

Seven
Residences and Streets

CORNER ORANGE AND LLEWELLYN ROADS, MONTCLAIR, N. J.

The Stephen Carey estate, near the corner of Llewellyn and Orange Roads, was named "Brooklawn" both because of Nashuayne Brook running at its edge and the wide expanse of lawn on its hillside. Mr. Carey purchased the property in 1871, built a brownstone residence, and enclosed his land with picturesque fences and bridges. A decade later, Carey bought additional property known as "Riker's Woods" adjacent to his own. Shortly after buying it he offered the property to the town without cost. The offer was rejected because there was no legal precedent for the town to accept it. More than half a century later, in 1935, Carey's son sold the land to the town for $78,000. The wooded preserve is today's Carey's Woods. Stone walls that formed the entrance to the estate, one of which is shown on the card, still exist today.

In this early 1900s view along Llewellyn Road, a horse and carriage are passing the long stretch of fence enclosing the Carey property. Carey had strong views about transportation. Although he pledged his own resources to back the bond issue for the Montclair Railway, he was opposed to the granting of a trolley franchise. The trolley would later pass his estate.

Llewellyn Road is on the left, Orange Road is in the center, and Elm Street is in the foreground. The house situated within the triangle in the center of the card is extant while the one at the right no longer exists. Curiously, the stone steps at the curbside leading to the latter still remain. One of the trolley rails in Elm Street can be seen at the bottom right.

CHILDREN'S HOME. GATES AVE., MONTCLAIR, N. J.

Dear Kyple, Do you expect to be in Somerville Christmas, if so dont forget to come over, couldnt begin to tell you how busy I am now. Sincerely Rose

The Children's Home, the first charitable institution in Montclair, was on Gates Avenue between Orange Road and Harrison Avenue. It was established in 1881 for the care of indigent children. Reverend Bradford was instrumental in its creation. The home (above left) opened in 1894, replacing a smaller building. Montclair Gardens occupies the site today.

Llewllyn Road and Residence of Wm. B. Dickson, Esq., Montclair N. J.

The William Brown Dickson estate occupied the entire block bounded by Llewellyn Road, Warren Place, Clinton Avenue, and Eagle Rock Way. Included on the property was a tennis court, greenhouse, and arbor. Mr. Dickson, an executive in the steel industry, was the driving force behind the creation of Montclair's parks.

Prospect Terrace, North of Hawthorne Place, Montclair, N. J.

Prospect Terrace was created in the 1890s. Toward the end of that decade, the two residences on the left were built. On the right, constructed in 1902 on land bounded by Prospect Terrace, Hawthorne Place, and Gates Avenue was a residence named "The Terraces." The inscription survives to this day in the leftmost of the pair of columns at its entrance.

Union Street from South Willow Street, Montclair, N. J.

The caption reads, "Union Street from South Willow Street." Referring to the arrows on this card mailed in 1908, the sender wrote, "This is our Louis's line of march every morning turning into Gates Avenue to the station." On his walk, Louis passed the Queen Anne-style home on the corner, then a decade old. It would win a Preservation Award in 1980.

SOUTH FULLERTON AVENUE, MONTCLAIR, N. J.

The house on the right, built in 1886 on the corner of South Fullerton Avenue and East Plymouth Street (Roosevelt Place today) has been owned by the same family for many years. Not altered, it retains its original decorative elements and is still separated from Roosevelt Place by the fence seen in the card. When constructed, a twin was built just south of it.

The Crescent, Montclair, N. J.

This view of The Crescent is looking east toward South Fullerton Avenue. When the second and third houses from the right were built in the late 1880s, Trinity Place did not exist and The Crescent curved south at its current western end and extended to Plymouth Street. It is likely that the shape of the street gave rise to its name.

89

Church Street, named for the Presbyterian church at its eastern end, was known as the "Old Road" until the early 1870s. The iron fence at the right enclosed the church on both its Bloomfield Avenue and Church Street sides. Ira Seymour Crane's home was on the left—near his Presbyterian church, hardware store, and the Montclair Savings Bank.

This c. 1905 view looks north on Valley Road from its intersection with Church Street. At the left is the grammar school, and at the right, just out of the picture, is the Carnegie Library. The garden would later be ringed by a low fence and is today the site of a circular fountain. It may be the smallest "rotary" in the state.

This photograph of the Clark home, located at 108 Orange Road, was on a postcard dated August 19, 1930, sent to Mrs. Sylvia Whitlock, Downing, Missouri. The message reads as follows: "Dear Sister—Just found some pictures of our house. Am sending you one. It is lovely here in Montclair. Hope all are well. Love to Wes. Sister Mary."

According to Montclair directories, Mary Clark lived in the house in 1929–30 but in 1931 the house was vacant. Around 1820, more than 100 years before Mary Clark sent this card, the first house at this location was built by Nathaniel Crane Jr. In 1863 the house became the retirement home of Dr. James Henry Clark, a prominent physician. The house in the photograph was constructed in 1894 by Dr. Clark's son, and the earlier house, without its kitchen, was moved to the rear of the site for use as a carriage house. Descendants of Dr. Clark occupied the house until 1962, nearly a century after it was purchased by Dr. Clark. The Clark House is now owned by the Montclair Historical Society and contains its administrative offices, classrooms, and the Terhune Library. The earlier structure, donated to the Montclair Historical Society in 1976, was later moved to the rear of the Israel Crane House, next door at 110 Orange Road. It is now "The Country Store."

Orange Road from Myrtle Avenue, Montclair, N. J.

An early 1900s view of Orange Road looks north from its intersection with Myrtle Avenue. The house at the right was at 77 Orange Road. On the card, mailed September 4, 1909, two days before Labor Day, was the timeless message, "Have already begun to look forward to next summer. Mary."

This residence at 65 Orange Road was located two houses north of the house at the top of the page. Both houses were razed when the Cranetown garden apartments were built between Church Street and Myrtle Avenue. After the apartments were constructed, Myrtle Avenue east of Orange Road ceased to exist except for a short piece west of Trinity Place.

South Mountain Avenue is depicted looking north from Myrtle Avenue. The house on the corner, built in 1900, featured a porte cochere on its north side and a deck with a balustrade. Postcards from the early 1900s always show the house with awnings; first blue and white, then red and white.

The Frederick Taylor Gates Mansion, completed in 1902, is on South Mountain Avenue west of Hillside Avenue. Built on 4 acres and containing 20 rooms, it was designed by George Washington Maher, a colleague of Frank Lloyd Wright. Gates was a Baptist minister who later became a financial adviser to John D. Rockefeller.

The Lloyd Road residence at the left, designed by Alfred F. Norris, was built in 1905. Features included curved gables and a turret with prominent finial. In 1907, E.J. Hoyt wrote, "Dear Cora, This is where I'm staying this summer. We can see N.Y. from our front porch. Regards to your people." E.J. was staying at 40 Lloyd Road, just out of the picture.

This card and the one preceding it were part of a series published by the Temme Company of Newark but printed in Germany. Mailed August 23, 1909, the view is from the corner of Lloyd Road and Hoburg Place. In the distance is the Church of the Immaculate Conception, seemingly without a cross, before its dedication on September 26, 1909.

THE MOUNTAINSIDE FROM AFTERGLOW WAY, MONTCLAIR, N. J.

"Casa Deldra" was built in 1912 on Afterglow Way. Constructed on the eastern slope of First Mountain, the unique residence occupies the northwest corner of its property. Also designed by architect Alfred F. Norris, it, too, features elaborately curved gables. The Hotel Montclair can be seen to the upper left in the background.

E. MADISON CO.   MOUNTAIN TOP NORTH OF BLOOMFIELD AVENUE, MONTCLAIR, N.J.

The card shows Bloomfield Avenue in the foreground, Lloyd Road to its left, and Parkhurst Place in the center. Today, The Montclair Kimberley Academy is on the site of the homes at the left. The residence at the top of the mountain was in Verona. On the right, the two homes farther up the mountainside are on the unseen Rockledge Road.

95

Based on the absence of landscaping, this view was probably captured soon after Rockledge Road was cut through around 1905. The residence with a turret in Verona again appears, this time near the left of the card. Except for a different canopy, the appearance of the house at the center of the card is today little changed from the early 1900s.

ROCKLEDGE ROAD

The house at the top of the page on the right is shown in this pre-1940 view, which again includes the Hotel Montclair. At some point in the three decades after the house was built, the open porches were enclosed and additions made. Although curbing has been installed, the road was not yet paved.

Situated near Montclair's business district, the house was on the west side of Park Street, roughly in the middle of the block between Bloomfield Avenue and Portland Place. Facing south, its long axis was perpendicular to Park Street. At the top left of the card is the caption, "One of Montclair's Oldest Houses, Mountain Ridge Studio 24 Park Street." The sign at the right reads, "Mountain Ridge Studio Miss Edith Felton." Never mailed, the card has no postmark.

It is questionable whether the house was ever one of Montclair's oldest. In addition to its appearance, there is no structure at 24 Park Street on an 1890 map. It is possible, however, that the house existed at a different location and was later moved to Park Street.

On December 28, 1944, a photograph of the house appeared on the front page of the *Montclair Times*. The headline above the photograph read, "How Park Street Looked in Winter of 1902" and the caption stated that in 1902 the house was owned by Charles Thomas. The house was later razed and in 1925 Elks Lodge 89 built their new home at this location. In the 1930s the Banker's National Life Insurance Company began occupying the former Elk's home. Today it is the Technopulp Building.

Fullerton Ave. from Munn St., Montclair, N. J.

This photograph was taken looking north on North Fullerton Avenue from Munn Street. North Fullerton Avenue was created in the 1870s and in the following decade Munn Street was extended east to join it. The porch of the house on the corner is now enclosed, a common alteration as air conditioning became commonplace.

Park St. corner Claremont Ave, Montclair, N. J.

#70 Park St is marked x

The residence on the left at the corner of Park Street and Claremont Avenue, built for Frederick J. Drescher, was completed in 1890. A carriage house at the northwest corner of the property was accessible either from Claremont Avenue or from Park Street by passing through the porte cochere at the right of the Drescher home.

98

Midland Ave. from Claremont Ave., Montclair, N. J.

Built in 1899, the residence at the right is on the east side of Midland Avenue north of Claremont Avenue. For the first quarter of the 1900s it was the home of Dr. John Raleigh Mott and his family. Dr. Mott, a leader in the YMCA, was a co-winner of the Nobel Peace Prize in 1946.

No. Mountain Ave., north from Claremont, Montclair, N. J.

Mailed in 1909, this card shows North Mountain Avenue looking north from Claremont Avenue. The third house from the left, built in 1797, was originally located a short distance south on the corner. It was purchased by Joseph Van Vleck in the 1860s for his first home. Van Dyk Manor, built in 1968, now occupies the site of the two houses on the left.

Hillside View, Montclair, N. J.   823

The "Hillside View" is near the intersection of Claremont and Upper Mountain Avenues. To the left of the houses, west of Upper Mountain Avenue, the top of the railroad cut leading to the never completed tunnel is visible. Today, Upper Mountain Gardens occupies the site of the two houses in the center of the card.

Scene on Mountain Slope, Montclair, N. J.

"Scene on Mountain Slope" looks west to the intersection of Claremont and Prospect Avenues. Both houses on the latter are extant as is the residence farther west on Claremont Avenue, now the Montclair Manor. It is possible the property at the right is vacant because of the bore beneath it for the railroad tunnel.

It is likely that this card, while never mailed, was sent as part of other correspondence. The message reads, "Holiday greetings from the Steele family at their new home 'Buena Vista' 42 Highland Avenue Montclair N.J. Built during the summer and occupied Oct 15/21."

BRUNSWICK ROAD.   MONTCLAIR, N. J.

When this card was mailed in 1926, these Brunswick Road homes were across the street from the Montclair Athletic Club. The absence of mature trees contrasts sharply with today's scene, particularly with the large weeping willow that now shades the first house on the right.

101

[handwritten text] elgin thanks for young and som's greetings from lake Minnewaska (in which my niece from *...*

The photograph of this Upper Mountain Avenue residence was taken between 1905 and 1910. Located just south of Edgewood Road, it was the home of photographer Henry A. Strohmeyer in the early years of the twentieth century. Privately printed, it is likely that he took this photograph of his home. Behind the house, at the crest of the mountain, is Kip's Castle.

The Castle, Montclair, N. J.

The construction of Kip's Castle began in 1902 and was finished in 1905. When completed, the castle was totally in Montclair. A later realignment of the Montclair-Verona border placed the western side of the building, shown above, in Verona. Originally called Kipsburg, it was built for Frederick and Charlotte Kip on 15 acres at an elevation of 665 feet.

The above mansion "On the Mountain" was built around 1910 for James Newbegin Jarvie. Known as the "coffee king," Jarvie was in the coffee importing and sugar refining businesses. He also was one of the original trustees of the Montclair Art Museum. In addition to the large, symmetric mansion with both front and side porches, the estate included a carriage house at the rear of the property. Mr. Jarvie died in 1929 in his mid-70s while sailing to England for a vacation. The homestead was left to his sister along with an annual income to maintain it. A fire, probably occurring in the 1930s, destroyed the home, and the property remained vacant for many years.

When the writer first came into possession of this card, the concrete wall and the street number 150 on the left column provided clues to the Upper Mountain Avenue location of the former Jarvie residence. Built on the site was, according to real estate listings at the time, "Montclair's landmark Oriental-inspired contemporary estate." The unique house, using part of its predecessor's foundation, was built in 1962. Around the corner, on Edgewood Road, the former Jarvie carriage house is now a private home.

Waterbury Road, Marlboro Park, Montclair, N. J.

848

I am having a fine time.
Carmen

Marlboro Park, developed by the Montclair Realty Company starting in 1897, roughly consisted of property along Watchung Avenue and Fairfield Street between Grove Street and the railroad. Properties on the eastern side of Montclair Avenue north of Fairfield Street were also part of Marlboro Park. The sales office was on Watchung Avenue opposite Waterbury Road and later relocated to the store now occupied by Town House Liquors in Watchung Plaza. The company's advertisement for homes on Waterbury Road read as follows. "MODERN HOUSES, of best construction and thoroughly up-to-date, located in beautiful 'MARLBORO PARK', near the center of the latest and best development of MONTCLAIR. FOR SALE at prices ranging from $8,000 upwards. Also a large variety of CHOICE BUILDING LOTS and villa sites in same section and elsewhere at very MODERATE PRICES AND ON REASONABLE TERMS. Whether seeking AN IDEAL HOME or a SAFE AND PROFITABLE REAL ESTATE INVESTMENT you will surely find no better opportunities than in the rapidly growing, purely residential 'PARK STREET SECTION' of New York's most charming suburb."

Accompanying the advertisement was a photograph very similar to that of the above card. The house at the left, at the corner of Watchung Avenue and Waterbury Road, was built in 1900; the building at the extreme right was constructed two years later.

104

This view of Watchung Avenue is looking toward Upper Mountain Avenue from west of Valley Road. As late as 1875 this portion of Watchung Avenue did not exist as the road ran west only to Valley Road. By 1890 Watchung Avenue had been cut through but its only house was on the corner of, and faced, Valley Road. The fence in the card enclosed that property.

Watchung Avenue is seen from the same location a few years later in a different season. The house on the right, constructed in 1902, was built near a well and pumping station that provided Montclair's first public water supply in 1887. The other houses on the right were also built during the first decade of the twentieth century.

Edgemont Road, Upper Montclair, N. J.

In 1906 Edgemont Road ran from Watchung Avenue to just north of Brookfield Road with house numbers on the southern end in the single digits. The double-gabled house on the right is north of Brookfield Road. Built around 1903, it is one of the earliest houses on Edgemont Road.

Edgemont Road, Upper Montclair, N. J.

These homes on Edgemont Road are south of Brookfield Road. In the days before air conditioning, awnings were a means of keeping houses cooler in the summer and also provided a degree of privacy on the front porch. In 1914 the sender of this card wrote, "This is a good example of most of the streets here. It is a very pretty place."

Brookfield Road, toward Mountain, Upper Montclair, N. J.

Här är gatan jag arbetar på
är det är inte vackert.

These residences on Brookfield Road are west of Edgemont Road. Several parcels of land at the eastern end of Brookfield Road are vacant in this *c.* 1910 scene, although there is a house on the northwest corner. The first visible house on the right was built around 1902. The message, in Swedish, says, "Here is the street I work on. Isn't it beautiful."

Godfrey Road, Upper Montclair, N. J.

By 1915 sidewalks had been installed on Godfrey Road but the street had not yet been paved. Tree planting was the responsibility of the Village Improvement Association, organized in 1878. Membership was open to residents who either planted a tree or paid a modest annual fee. Elms and Norway maples were among the trees suggested for planting.

The ladies in white will soon be at Watchung Avenue on their late afternoon stroll along Upper Mountain Avenue. The Tudor residence on the left was constructed in 1897 while the one on the right, one of the oldest on Upper Mountain Avenue, was built in 1878. North of the lamppost, a private road provided access to the carriage houses for both homes.

According to the back of the undated card, and confirmed by a 1930 Montclair Directory, this Cooper Avenue residence between Park and Grove Streets was "Frank and Josie Reed's house." Except for a wider dormer, the house today remains basically unchanged.

In this post-1907 scene, the auto is at the intersection of Bellevue and North Mountain Avenues. In the late 1800s the latter was named Cliffside Avenue. At the top left was the home of Charles W. Anderson. At the bottom left is Anderson Park, created on the land Mr. Anderson donated to Montclair and taken into the Essex County Park System in 1903.

The writer of this card lived at the eastern end of Garfield Place and from his home could see the two residences across the street on Valley Road. He appeared to like Montclair for he wrote, "It is too lovely for description up here and no need to go farther except to see the ocean." The southbound trolley which passed his home could have started such a trip.

This card was mailed on June 21, 1921.

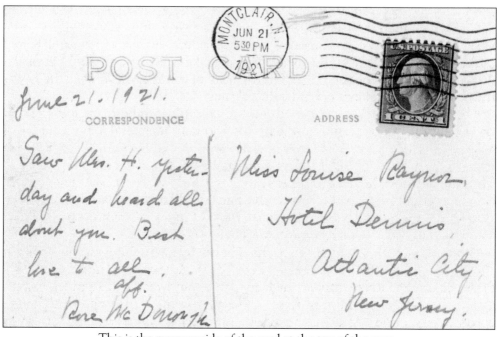

This is the message side of the card at the top of the page.

A Note Concerning Rose McDonough

The postcard on the preceding page was of particular interest to the writer because of the hundreds of Montclair cards in his possession, only two of them had messages written by the same person—Rose McDonough. The card at the left was of greater interest since it was possible that it was Rose McDonough's home. The only facts were the Montclair postmark, the date June 21, 1921, and the name of the sender. It was likely, given the postmark, that the house was in Montclair, but not necessarily.

The first step was to find, if it still existed, the house itself. A 1930 Montclair Directory stated that Rose S. McDonough, musician, lived at 157 Christopher Street. A trip to 157 Christopher Street found that the house still existed and was little changed from the 1921 postcard. The address itself would prove to be the key to unlocking other sources of information. Expecting only to find information that confirmed what was in the directory, the writer went to the tax assessor's office at the Montclair Municipal Building and asked to see the deeds for 157 Christopher Street. On the back of the last McDonough deed was the date of Rose McDonough's death, February 16, 1956.

The obituary for Rose, obtained from a microfilm of the *Montclair Times* at the Montclair Public Library, stated that she had been a lifelong resident of Montclair until she went to live with her niece in Connecticut. Rose died one year later at the age of 78. Her parents were Thomas and Mary Oakley McDonough and her grandfather was Commodore Thomas MacDonough, commander of U.S. naval forces at the Battle of Plattsburg, New York, in the War of 1812. She was survived by a brother Rodney of North Caldwell. Rose was buried in the Mount Hebron cemetery.

While at the library, the writer thought there might be some information about 157 Christopher Street. There was. Researchers from the 1982 Preservation Montclair project had uncovered and recorded significant facts about the house. Based on Essex County records and maps, the house, constructed around 1865, was the oldest residence on Christopher Street. It was built by Thomas McDonough, Rose's father, who owned 48 acres of land in the area. When built, however, Christopher Street did not exist and the front of the house faced Grove Street, one block to the east. As late as 1890 a map of Montclair showed that Christopher Street ran only as far north as Chestnut Street. The map also showed a path from the McDonough home running southeast to Grove Street. On a later 1906 map, Christopher Street is shown extending to Watchung Avenue. McDonough Street, named after the family, also appears, slightly to the north of their home.

Several months later, an inquiry was made at Mount Hebron Cemetery as to Rose's final place of rest. A map was appropriately marked. Walking down one of the paths the writer was joined by William McElroy, the general manager of the cemetery. Within a few minutes the McDonough family grave site was reached. The family monument faced the road and Rose, Rodney, and their family were nearby.

After a few minutes, Mr. McElroy said there were was much to be learned within the cemetery. A short distance south of the McDonough grave site was the grave of Herman Hupfeld. The writer, who had never heard of Mr. Hupfeld, was told that he was a composer who had lived on Park Street. Of greater significance, he had written the words and music to one of America's best known love songs, "As Time Goes By." Perhaps too quickly.

Eight
Scenes around Town

Truck No. 1, M. F. D , Montclair, N J

Mailed in 1907, this card depicts the apparatus of Truck Company Number 1 being pulled up Bloomfield Avenue by a team of three horses. The building directly behind the horses contained the butcher store of Henry L. Dunning, who, according to his sign, sold "Choice Meats." Behind the truck, the three-story brick building is currently occupied by The Office while the structure at the far corner of Midland Avenue is now the Zaentz Hardware-Houseware store. The men, horses, and equipment are returning to headquarters just up the street on the corner of Valley Road (p. 34). It would not be until 1912 that Truck Company Number 1 would receive a motorized vehicle to replace its horse-drawn truck.

Hose Co. No. 2, Montclair Fire Department.

Excelsior Hose Company Number 2, organized on March 24, 1887, to serve the south end of Montclair, was originally located at Orange Road and Cedar Avenue. The company initially consisted of 20 unpaid volunteers and was the first to have a person on duty 24 hours a day. For the first five years of its operation the company used a hand carriage propelled by its members. In 1892, a hose cart and horse were purchased from the Newark Fire Department, making it the fire company the first in Montclair to use a horse to pull its equipment. The station above, a one-door structure on the corner of Harrison and Cedar Avenues, was built in 1901. By 1914 the entire fire department was on a paid basis and three years later all of Montclair's horse-drawn apparatus had been replaced by motorized vehicles.

HOSE COMPANY NO. 3, MONTCLAIR N. J.

Just back from the Hoboken fire —
Pryor saved.

Washington Hose Company Number 3, organized on August 9, 1887, had their first station at the corner of Bloomfield Avenue and Grove Street. In those early years, members provided the necessary funds for its horses, apparatus, and station house furnishings. The second station (shown above) was erected in 1893 on Bloomfield Avenue between Elm and Hartley Streets. Shortly before construction of the station began the company was presented with a horse from George Inness Jr. and also a hose wagon from the township committee. In those pre-electronic years, the megaphones seen in the group picture were used for voice amplification at the site of a fire. The Crawford Crews American Legion Post 251 has owned the building since 1944.

The message on the card, "Just back from the Hoboken fire—Pryor saved" arouses interest. The card, addressed to Miss Cora Benson and postmarked August 15, 1905, is not signed by the sender. Possibly he was one of the men in the picture. In all likelihood, the fire refers to the conflagration at the Hoboken station and ferry slips of the Delaware, Lackawanna and Western Railroad that began the evening of August 7, 1905. The slips and station were destroyed and the station that replaced it is the one that exists today. "Pryor" remains a mystery.

UPPER MONTCLAIR, FIRE DEPARTMENT, No. 4.

F. W. Poecker, Stationer.

Organized on February 7, 1888, Cliffside Hose Company Number 4 was originally located on the south side of Bellevue Avenue just west of the Erie Railroad tracks. In 1902, the above two-door brownstone station on Valley Road just north of Cooper Avenue was completed. The horses posed in the picture were trained to gallop to the front of their wagon when the alarm rang. In 1997 the door and opening on the right were slightly enlarged to accommodate a new ladder truck. The removed stones were retained for future use if the need ever arose to restore the station to its original appearance.

Hart's Livery was on Cooper Avenue just east of Valley Road. Built in 1903 by John Hart, a salesman, it also functioned as a pickup-delivery service and a storage facility. In 1904 Hart's was one of 12 liveries in Montclair. Another was Commonwealth Stables on Valley Road that occupied the building now used by Talbots.

Cooper Avenue, Upper Montclair, N. J.

The front of the first floor of Hart's Livery contained carriages while the rear contained stables. A hand-operated elevator utilizing a rope and pulley was used to move goods between the ground floor and the storage area on the second floor. Around 1950, the building was purchased by the Johnson Organ Company, which sold it in 1979. At that time the interior was adapted for office use. In the early 1990s the horse stalls and mangers were removed, partitioned offices were created, and the building was renovated and named The Livery. A window has replaced the entrance at the right of the building and cement now covers the front facade.

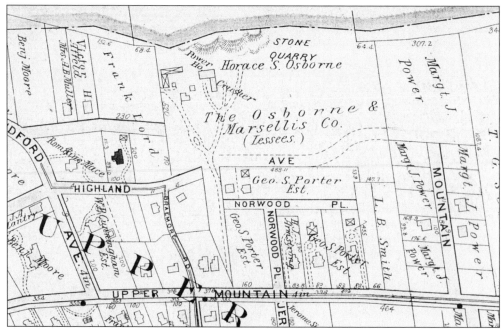

The Osborne and Marsellis traprock quarry was located at the crest of First Mountain near the western end of today's Edgecliff Road. A supplier of crushed stone, coal, lumber, and mason's material, the company built many of Montclair's roads. Its offices and storage facilities were located south of Bellevue Avenue slightly east of the railroad.

The quarrying operation relied on steam power to remove the traprock from the face of First Mountain presumably by drilling. At the base of the cliff the traprock was moved to the crusher via horse-drawn carts. The broken stone was then either taken to the company's storage facilities or directly to a construction site. Operations stopped in the 1920s and Edgecliff Road was extended westward to the Cedar Grove border. The area's heritage is recalled by the name given to the later extension of the street in Cedar Grove—Old Quarry Road.

Birdseye View of Upper Montclair, N. J.

The view is of the north side of Bellevue Avenue east of the railroad. Behind the stores, the outbuildings and field were part of the Van Gieson property. According to tradition, an effigy of the Kaiser was burned twice in this field near the end of World War I. The first burning occurred as a result of a false armistice, the second for the actual end to the war.

Park View, Montclair, N. J.

Montclair's first park was the small triangular parcel north of the Bloomfield Avenue railroad station that was purchased from the Crane estate. The second was the 14-acre Anderson Park, shown here before paths were created and landscaping undertaken. The Erie Railroad can be seen to the lower right.

This card of Anderson Park was mailed in 1906. On a plaque fastened to a boulder near the northeast corner of the park is the following inscription, "The lands comprising this park were donated to the town of Montclair by Charles W. Anderson for the purposes of a public park and in June 1903, it was taken into the Essex County Park System."

This "Bird's Eye View of Upper Montclair" is from the early 1900s. In the foreground is Anderson Park and on the other side of the railroad tracks are the storage facilities for the Osborne and Marsellis Company. Today's road leading to Upper Montclair Plaza was Osborne Place in the 1930s. At the center of the card is Cooper Avenue.

Edgemont Park, Montclair, N. J.

Charles Anderson's generosity was the impetus behind the creation of the Citizen's Park Committee. Formed to acquire future parkland, one of its recommended purchases was the Harrison Tract Park (later renamed Edgemont), west of Valley Road. In April of 1906 a referendum was held, and passed, on the issuing of $100,000 in bonds for land acquisition.

18:—SCENE IN EDGEMONT PARK, MONTCLAIR, N. J.

William B. Dickson, a steel industry executive and Llewellyn Road resident (p. 87), spearheaded the drive to pass the referendum on Montclair parks. Dickson's involvement included his personal subscription to $25,000 of the $100,000 bond issue. A memorial in honor of Mr. Dickson is on the western side of the pond in Edgemont Park.

121

The World War Memorial in Edgemont Park, dedicated in 1925, bears the following inscription: "In Grateful Tribute To The Men Of Montclair Who In the World War Paid the Last Full Measure of Devotion in Defense of the American Principles of Liberty and Justice For All." Tablets honoring those who served in World War II, Korea, and Vietnam were later added.

The current Montclair High School at Chestnut and Park Streets opened in late 1915. Two years later, the outdoor amphitheater, a gift from Florence Rand Lang (benefactor of the Montclair Art Museum), opened with a concert. It is still used for summer musical events and graduation exercises.

Rand Park, Montclair, New Jersey

Rand Park, at the corner of Chestnut and Park Streets, was a gift in 1918 of Mrs. Annie Rand (mother of Florence Rand Lang) in memory of her husband Jasper R. Rand. Mr. Rand, an inventor, was in the business of manufacturing drilling equipment. His company later became part of the Ingersoll-Rand Corporation.

Arch Bridge, Glenfield Park, Montclair, N. J.

The 1906 referendum on parks involved land that would later become Edgemont Park, Glenfield Park, Nishuane Park, and Woodman Field. At the time of voting, the future Glenfield Park (shown above), had already been subdivided and some housing erected. It was this acquisition that received the greatest plurality.

Mountainside Hospital, Montclair, N. J.

Mountainside Hospital opened its doors in 1891 in a rented cottage on the northwest corner of Highland Avenue and today's Bay Street. Two years later, a new building on Highland Avenue, shown at the right, added 36 beds and the first operating room to the hospital. A later surgical facility (on the left) opened in 1905.

Mountainside Hospital
Montclair N.J.

The above photograph of Mountainside was taken before the west wing was added in 1931. The sign, readable from Bay Avenue, states "No Parking Inside These Premises." Valet parking had not yet come of age. Mountainside's name is attributed to Dr. Amory Bradford, who suggested it because the founding committee members came from towns on both sides of Watchung Mountain.

The Essex County Park Commission, established in 1895, was the first such organization in the country. At the suggestion of Llewellyn Haskell (the developer of Llewellyn Park in West Orange), the commissioners purchased land from West Orange, Verona, and Montclair to create Eagle Rock Reservation. The entrance to the reservation is on Undercliff Road.

WINDING ROAD TO EAGLE ROCK, N. J.

The "Winding Road to Eagle Rock" from Montclair, included, then and now, several hairpin turns creating a road much akin to a railroad switchback. The tortuous path leads to the top of First Mountain with an elevation of over 600 feet. Bald eagles on the mountain's eastern side in the early nineteenth century gave the area its name.

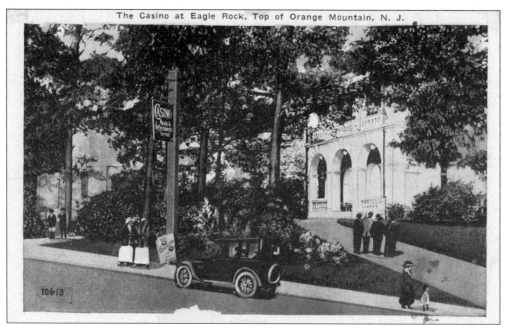

10613

The Casino at Eagle Rock, completed in 1911, originally served as a refreshment stand and rest area. Never used for gambling, the name came from its prominent arches, as shown in this card from the 1920s. The sign near the top of the postcard reads, "CASINO Meals & Refreshments Served," and the one beneath it reads, "Hot Chocolate."

CASINO CREST DRIVE, EAGLE ROCK RESERVATION

In this late 1940s view, the signs and socializing are gone and will soon be replaced by graffiti and decay. By the early 1980s the building was not only unattractive but hazardous as well. The casino's fortunes were soon reversed when work began on a two-year reconstruction project which culminated in the opening of Highlawn Pavilion in December of 1986.

Eagle Rock, Top of Orange Mountain.

The lookout at Eagle Rock provides a panoramic view to the east and was used by Washington's troops to monitor the movements of the British during the Revolution. In this card, mailed in 1908 when carriages were still prevalent, the writer asked, "Do you remember looking off from the top of this when you were here?"

People on Eagle Rock, Top of Orange Mountain.

The view from Eagle Rock has been a source of pleasure and inspiration for centuries. Whether gazing at the cities beyond or the towns below, the accomplishments of past generations of thinkers and builders are evident. In that sense, as William Faulkner wrote, "The past is never dead. It's not even past."

Select Bibliography

Carlisle, Robert D.B. *A Jewel in the Suburbs: The Montclair Art Museum*. Montclair, NJ: Montclair Art Museum, 1982.

Carlisle, Robert D.B. *The Montclair Golf Club: A Way of Life 1893–1983*. Montclair, NJ: The Montclair Golf Club, 1984.

Carlisle, Robert D.B. *Within These Halls: 1887–1987 The Montclair Kimberley Academy*. Montclair, NJ: The Montclair Kimberley Academy, 1988.

Central Presbyterian Church. *Central Sesquicentennial 1837–1987*. Montclair, NJ: Central Presbyterian Church, 1987.

Doremus, Philip. *Reminiscences of Montclair: With Some Account of Montclair's Part in the Civil War*. Montclair, NJ: Privately Published, 1908.

Dorflinger, Don. "Caldwell Branch Memories—Part 1." Block Line: *Tri-State Chapter Newsmagazine* June 1982: 16–24.

Goodell, Edwin B. *Montclair: The Evolution of a Suburban Town*. Montclair, NJ: The Edward Madison Company, 1934.

Harris, General F. H. *An Historical Sketch of Montclair: From its Earliest Settlement to the Centennial Anniversary of National Independence*. Montclair, NJ: Montclair Times, 1881.

Montclair Board of Education. *Then and Now in Public Education in Montclair*. Montclair, NJ: 1930.

Montclair Centennial Publicity Committee. *Montclair: The First 100 Years*. Montclair, NJ: 1968.

Montclair 125th Anniversary Book Committee. *Montclair 1868–1993*. Montclair, NJ: Township of Montclair, 1994.

Preservation Montclair. *Montclair Inventory of Historic, Cultural, and Architectural Resources*. Montclair, NJ: Junior League Montclair-Newark, 1982.

Riley, John Harrington. *The Newark City Subway Lines*. Oak Ridge, NJ: John Harrington Riley, 1987.

Roorda, Garrett C. *The Little Stone Church on Cow Pasture Corner*. Privately Published, 1996.

Sons of the American Revolution, New Jersey Society, Montclair Chapter. *The Story of Montclair: Its People in Peace and War Times*. Montclair, NJ: 1930.

Watkins, S.C.G., D.D.S. *Reminiscences of Montclair*. New York, NY: A.S. Barnes and Company, 1929.

Whittemore, Henry. *History of Montclair Township*. New York, NY: The Suburban Publishing Company, 1894.